# RAIN FOREST ANIMAL ADAPTATIONS

by Lisa J. Amstutz

Content Consultant
Jackie Gai, DVM
Zoo and Exotic Animal Consultation

CAPSTONE PRESS
a capstone imprint

A+ Books are published by Capstone Press,
1710 Roe Crest Drive, North Mankato, Minnesota 56003.
www.capstonepub.com

Copyright © 2012 by Capstone Press, a Capstone imprint.
All rights reserved.
No part of this publication may be reproduced in whole or in part, or stored in a retrieval system,
or transmitted in any form or by any means, electronic, mechanical, photocopying, recording,
or otherwise, without written permission of the publisher.
For information regarding permission, write to Capstone Press,
1710 Roe Crest Drive, North Mankato, Minnesota 56003.

*Library of Congress Cataloging-in-Publication Data*
Amstutz, Lisa J.
  Rain forest animal adaptations / By Lisa J. Amstutz.
    p. cm.—(A+ books amazing animal adaptations)
  Includes bibliographical references and index.
  Summary: "Simple text and photographs describe rain forest animal adaptations"—Provided by publisher.
  ISBN 978-1-4296-6028-0 (library binding)—ISBN 978-1-4296-7034-0 (pbk.)
  1. Rain forest animals—Adaptation—Juvenile literature.  I. Title. II. Series.
  QL112.A67 2012
  591.734—dc22                                                             2011004819

**Credits**
Jeni Wittrock, editor; Matt Bruning and Gene Bentdahl, designers;
    Wanda Winch, media researcher

**Photo Credits**
DigitalVision (Getty Images), cover (middle), 24; Dreamstime: Lawrence Wee, 16, Wouter Tolenaars, 13; iStockphoto: Himagine, 14; James P. Rowan, 8, 9; Nature Picture Library: Anup Shah, 19, Jouan & Rius, 18, PREMAPHOTOS/Ken Preston-Mafham, 25, Staffan Widstrand, 23, Sue Daly, 12; Shutterstock: Evgeniy Ayupov, 28, file404, Design Element, fivespots, 21, Ivalin, 4, Sebastian Duda, 1, silver-john, cover (fern), STILLFX, Design Element, worldswildlifewonders, 17; SuperStock, Inc.: Animals Animals, 6, imagebroker.net, 22, Tier und Naturfotografie, 10, 26, Tom Brakefield, 27; Visuals Unlimited, Inc.: Thomas Marent, 20

**Note to Parents, Teachers, and Librarians**
The Amazing Animal Adaptations series uses full color photographs and a nonfiction format to introduce the concept of animal adaptations. *Rain Forest Animal Adaptations* is designed to be read aloud to a pre-reader or to be read independently by an early reader. Photographs help listeners and early readers understand the text and concepts discussed. The book encourages further learning by including the following sections: Table of Contents, Glossary, Read More, Internet Sites, and Index. Early readers may need assistance using these features.

# TABLE OF CONTENTS

Life in the Forest .................. 4
Body Coverings .................. 6
Body Parts ........................ 15
Behavior .......................... 24

Glossary ........................... 30
Read More ........................ 31
Internet Sites ................... 31
Index ............................... 32

# Life in the Forest

Tropical rain forests are hot, steamy places. Most receive 100 inches (254 centimeters) of rain each year.

Rain forest animals have special ways to stay safe, find food, and find mates. These ways are called "adaptations."

# Body Coverings

In the rain forest, light flickers through the trees. The jaguar's spots help it hide in the shadowy leaves. Spots camouflage the cat as it hunts deer.

This chameleon's leafy green color hides it from hungry birds. A fly may not see it either ... until it's too late. The lizard's long, sticky tongue will shoot out. Good-bye, fly!

The Malaysian orchid mantis mimics a flower. If an insect stops by for some dinner, surprise! The mantis will eat him for dinner instead.

The rain forest is a giant place. Some rain forest animals use bright colors to help find each other. The rainbow feathers of a scarlet macaw attract a mate from far away.

Sometimes bright colors mean danger. The golden poison-dart frog is one of the deadliest animals in the world. The poison in one frog could kill 100 people.

The poisonous Queen Alexandra's birdwing butterfly grows as big as a dinner plate. Poison from the vines it eats stays in its body. Its bright color warns birds to stay away.

High in the treetops, the sloth hangs upside down by its claws. In fact, its hair grows upside down too! Rainwater runs right off.

15

# Body Parts

Some animals have special bodies for traveling through the rain forest. A paradise tree snake can flatten its body like a ribbon. It glides from tree to tree.

A harpy eagle's wings are short and broad. It easily twists and turns through the trees, hunting monkeys.

Geckos have tiny, sticky hairs on their feet. These hairs help them hold onto wet, slippery branches and leaves.

Small size helps mouse deer slip easily through brush on the forest floor. They are not much bigger than house cats.

A spider monkey uses its tail as an extra arm. It swings from branch to branch. Wouldn't it be handy to have an extra arm?

A green tree python wraps its tail around branches too. Then it can reach down to snatch a passing bird or mouse.

It is hard to reach food high up in a tree. Okapis pull off leaves and fruit with their long tongues. They can even lick their own eyelids.

The toucan has a long beak. It can reach a lizard or piece of fruit far out on a branch.

23

# Behavior

Many rain forest animals stick together. Gorillas live in family groups. They help each other protect their young.

Millions of army ants march together on the rain forest floor. This army is small but fierce. It will attack anything in its path.

Most cats hate water. But when the weather is hot, Sumatran tigers take a dip in a river. They are good swimmers.

A capybara family stays cool in the water too. Capybaras can swim under water for up to five minutes. They can even sleep in the water!

This chart shows rain forest adaptations mentioned in this book. Can you remember each animal's adaptation?

| Animal | Behavior | Body Covering | Body Parts |
|---|---|---|---|
| army ant | ● | | |
| capybara | ● | | |
| chameleon | | ● | |
| gecko | | | ● |
| golden poison-dart frog | | ● | |
| gorilla | ● | | |
| green tree python | | | ● |

| Animal | Behavior | Body Covering | Body Parts |
|---|---|---|---|
| harpy eagle | | | 🟢 |
| jaguar | | 🟢 | |
| Malaysian orchid mantis | | 🟢 | |
| mouse deer | | | 🟢 |
| okapi | | | 🟢 |
| paradise tree snake | | | 🟢 |
| Queen Alexandra's birdwing butterfly | | 🟢 | |
| scarlet macaw | | 🟢 | |
| sloth | | 🟢 | |
| spider monkey | | | 🟢 |
| sumatran tiger | 🟢 | | |
| toucan | | | 🟢 |

# Glossary

**adaptation**—a change a living thing goes through to better fit in with its environment

**attract**—to draw near

**camouflage**—to blend in with what's around you

**mate**—the male or female partner of a pair of animals

**mimic**—to copy

**tropical**—having to do with the hot and wet areas near the equator

# Read More

**Berkes, Marianne Collins**. *Over in the Jungle: A Rainforest Rhyme*. Sharing Nature with Children. Nevada City, Calif.: Dawn Publications, 2007.

**Salas, Laura Purdie**. *Rain Forests: Gardens of Green*. Amazing Science. Minneapolis: Picture Window Books, 2007.

**Underwood, Deborah**. *Hiding in Rain Forests*. Creature Camouflage. Chicago: Heinemann Library, 2011.

# Internet Sites

FactHound offers a safe, fun way to find Internet sites related to this book. All of the sites on FactHound have been researched by our staff.

Here's all you do:
Visit www.facthound.com
Type in this code: 9781429660280

Check out projects, games and lots more at
www.capstonekids.com

# Index

army ants, 25
camouflage, 6, 8
capybaras, 27
chameleons, 8
colors, 8, 10, 12, 13
geckos, 18
golden poison-dart frogs, 12
gorillas, 24
green tree pythons, 21
harpy eagles, 17
jaguars, 6
Malaysian orchid mantids, 9
mates, 10
monkeys, 17, 20
mouse deer, 19
okapis, 22
paradise tree snakes, 16
poisons, 12, 13
Queen Alexandra's birdwing butterflies, 13
scarlet macaws, 10
sloths, 15
Sumatran tigers, 26
toucans, 23